First Drawings
PEOPLE

ABDO
Publishing Company

A Buddy Book by Maria Hosley

VISIT US AT

www.abdopublishing.com

Published by ABDO Publishing Company, 4940 Viking Drive, Edina, Minnesota 55435.

Copyright © 2007 by Abdo Consulting Group, Inc. International copyrights reserved in all countries. No part of this book may be reproduced in any form without written permission from the publisher. Buddy Books™ is a trademark and logo of ABDO Publishing Company.

Printed in the United States.

Editor: Sarah Tieck
Contributing Editor: Michael P. Goecke
Graphic Design: Maria Hosley
Illustrations: Maria Hosley, Mary Unzelman
Interior Photographs: Photos.com

Library of Congress Cataloging-in-Publication Data

Hosley, Maria.
   People / Maria Hosley.
      p. cm. — (First drawings)
   Includes index.
   ISBN-13: 978-1-59679-812-0
   ISBN-10: 1-59679-812-2
   1. Human figure in art—Juvenile literature. 2. Pencil drawing—Technique—Juvenile literature. I. Title.

NC765.H673 2007
743.4—dc22

                                     2006034581

Table Of Contents

Getting Started

Today you're going to learn to draw people. Not sure you know how to draw? If you know how to make circles, squares, and triangles, you can draw most anything!

You will learn to draw in four steps. First, you will measure to get the correct sizes. Next, you will lightly draw the basic shapes. This helps you construct people. From those basic shapes, you will make the final outline. And last, you will erase the basic shape lines and add **detail**.

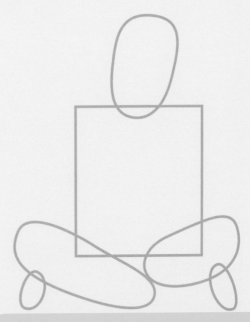

To draw people, you'll need paper, a sharpened pencil, a big eraser, and a hard, flat surface. Many artists like to draw at a table or a desk. They sit up straight with their tools in front of them. Gather your supplies. Then, let's get started!

ARTIST'S TOOLBOX

Some people are tall, some are short, some have red hair, and some have brown hair. But, most people have the same basic parts. These include one head, two arms, two hands, and so on. Some artists have folders filled with **reference** pictures of people! These pictures help them create their drawings.

Start your own folder by collecting photographs or pictures from magazines. Use them as you draw. This book has reference pictures to get you started.

Measurements and Proportions

Have you ever looked at a drawing and thought about whether it looks real? Many people draw things that look real.

To make a **realistic** drawing of a person, find the correct proportions. Proportion is the size of one thing compared to another. For example, a person's head should be a size that fits with his or her body. Using correct proportions helps make your people drawings look realistic.

There's an easy way to match the proportions of a person for your drawing. You can use strips of paper to measure the body parts on your **reference** picture. Here's how to do it:

Cut a strip of paper the same height as the girl's head. Then, make several more strips of the same size.

Lay the strips on the kids. Do this to compare the head size with the width and the height of the kids.

The height of the kids together is a little more than 5 strips.

The width is a little more than 4 strips.

Choosing A Size For Your Drawing

To draw these kids at this size, cut several strips of paper that match the length of the orange strips shown above.

If you want a larger drawing, cut longer strips. And if you want a smaller drawing, cut shorter strips. Just make sure the strips fit on your drawing paper.

Place your cut strips on your drawing paper.
Arrange them so they match the reference picture.
With your pencil, lightly mark the ends of each strip.

Add extra room here because the kids are a little wider than 4 strips.

Add extra room here because the kids are a little taller than 5 strips.

Basic Shapes

All things are easier to draw if you break them down into basic shapes. Draw these shapes *very lightly*. They are only a guide that you will erase later. And when the lines are light, it is easy to erase and try again. Remember to use your proportion lines as a guide!

Between your top guidelines, draw a tall oval for each head. Make an angled rectangle for the **torso** and tall rectangles for the legs. Draw long ovals for the arm parts. Last, **sketch** lines for the hands and the feet.

Leaving the strips on the reference picture will help you position your shapes.

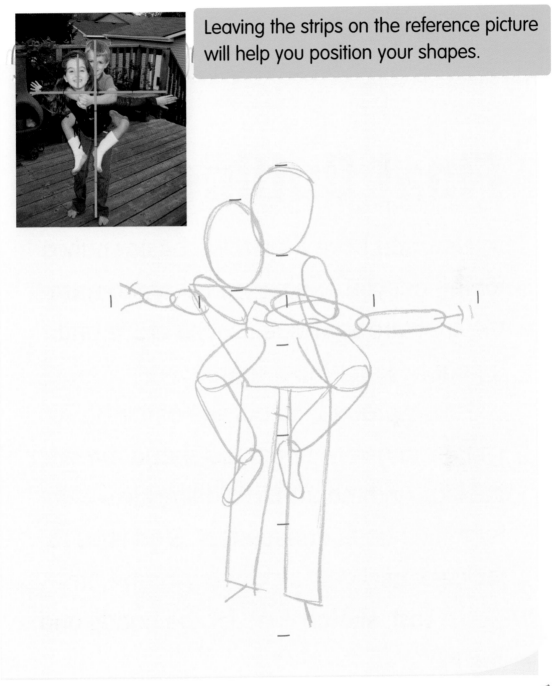

Final Outline

Now you have drawn the basic shapes for the people! You can use them to make the final outline shape. Do this *lightly* with a pencil.

Follow around the outside of the basic shapes to give your people shape. Draw the legs and the arms. Add lines to form the hands and the feet. Start lines to indicate hair.

Draw lines to crisscross the centers of the head ovals. You will use these lines to help position the nose, the mouth, and the eyes.

Adding Detail

Once you are happy with your outline, erase the basic shape lines. Be careful not to erase any lines you still need.

Now you can add the **details**! Fill in the hair. Draw some wrinkles and seams on the clothes. Finally, add shading.

A person's face and hands are easier to draw when you use guidelines. Study and practice the guides shown here. Then, finish your drawing.

Half

Half

Half

Half

Start with an oval as the basic shape for the head. Draw lines across and down the middle to divide the face into four parts.

Place the eyes in the middle of the oval. Place the nose halfway between the eyes and the oval bottom. Draw the bottom of the mouth halfway between the nose and the oval bottom.

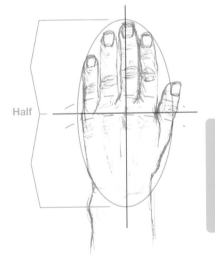

Half

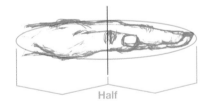

Half

When drawing a hand start with an oval. Draw the knuckles at the oval's halfway point. The tip of the middle finger should reach one end and the wrist should be at the other.

When you are happy with your outline and **details**, you can make them darker. Do this with your pencil or a marker. Erase any extra lines, and you're done!

Keep Drawing

You have now finished a drawing of people. Good job! Use these steps next time you want to draw something.

Don't worry if drawing feels like a challenge at first. Like anything else, drawing takes practice.

Have fun with your new skills. And remember to practice, practice, practice! The more you draw the better you will become.

Want to add to your drawing? Try using **charcoal** to add **texture** and character to your people drawing.

19

Use a charcoal
pencil to shade and
shape the people.

Caricature People

It is fun to **exaggerate** parts or features of people. This is how you make a caricature. A caricature is a picture that looks like a cartoon.

Choose one body part or feature of each person. Then, exaggerate it to make it look funny. Just use your imagination!

Practice drawing faces that show different emotions. Then, try making the body positions match each person's mood.

HOPEFUL

bored

unhappy

Using the same basic shapes, we created a caricature of the kids. We made the girl's eyes larger and added costumes. These details make the children look playful.

Important Words

charcoal a black material used for drawing.

detail a minor decoration, such as wrinkles.

exaggerate to make something seem larger than it really is.

realistic showing things as they are in real life.

reference a picture or an item used for information or help.

sketch to make a rough drawing.

texture the look and feel of something.

torso the human body, not including the head, arms, and legs.

Web Sites

To learn more about drawing people, visit ABDO Publishing Company on the World Wide Web. Web site links about drawing people are featured on our Book Links page. These links are routinely monitored and updated to provide the most current information available.

www.abdopublishing.com

Index